Nashaun Bassont

Bare Feet
and
Dirt Roads:
A Memoir in Two Parts

RACHAEL WOODALL

ISBN-10: 1543211127
ISBN-13: 978-1543211122

DEDICATION

For my Nana and her "smiling eyes"

CONTENTS

Acknowledgments   i

1   DEAR POPPA   5

2   THE BACKSTORY   10

3   POPPA WRITES   13

4   THE 1930S, COTTON PICKING AND OTHER ODD   19
    JOBS

5   A CHRISTMAS MIRACLE AND A HARD WINTER IN   25
    THE WILSON HOUSE

6   POPPA'S WORLD   33

7   DUCK FOR LUNCH, SQUIRREL FOR DINNER   39

8   TO THE PROMISED LAND   47

9   LOVE AND MARRIAGE GO TOGETHER   62

10 A FATEFUL CHANGE   69

11 BABY DAYS AND DREAMS OF THOUSANDS OF   79
    GALLONS OF MILK

12 A POEM   93

13 GOING WAY BACK: MATTIE'S STORY   96

14 FALLING IN LOVE   111

15 REAL LIFE AND RAISING A FAMILY   115

ACKNOWLEDGMENTS

Thank you to my grandfather, Charles Lowell, who penned his memoirs in 2002. We are so glad you wrote down your story. Thank you to my Great-Aunt Nobie, who first typed and edited his memoirs via countless handwritten letters. And thank you to Carol Kinsey, who told me it'd be worth my time. You were right.

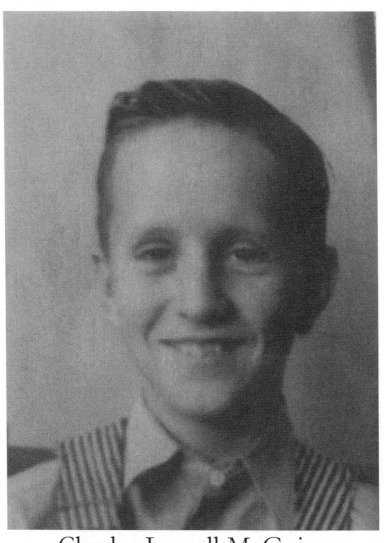

Charles Lowell McGuire
(1929 – 2012)

1

RACHAEL WOODALL

A BRIEF GENEAOLOGY

In the year 1911, Martha Ann gave birth to Edna Mae.

In the year 1929, Edna Mae gave birth to Charles Lowell.

In the year 1952, Margaret Clara gave birth to Vicki Lynn.

In the year 1980, Vicki Lynn gave birth to me, Rachael Christine.

RACHAEL WOODALL

1 DEAR POPPA

It's been so long since I've written. You've been gone now five years. I still miss getting letters from you. In your letters you would tell me about your travels with Nana. You asked me about my comings and goings. You taught me new words – so many spelling lessons! –and offered advice. I think of you often, sometimes wondering what you would tell me if you wrote to me today.

I know you'd ask about your great-grandkids, about our life in the Midwest. I wonder what you'd think of our world today in the 21st century. I would guess that the advances in technology now are beyond what was dreamed of in your day. But then again, perhaps you didn't dream of technology, because it didn't rule your life as it does ours. Relationships in your day were established in person, not by clicking or commenting on social media. News was communicated in person or in writing, not by way of hand-held computers the size of a billfold. Home phones are almost obsolete; my kids giggle at the thought of a phone attached to a cord and the wall.

Oh, Poppa, my kids would love you, and I know you would love them dearly. I remember you getting down on the floor and playing with them when they were babies and toddlers, pushing wooden trucks and trains, doing puzzles and blowing bubbles. I tell them about you often, stories you told me about growing up in Texas or adventures we had together when I was a child.

Great-nana sends the kids care packages every month. They love her from afar and know she loves them.

Today we are busy hurrying from one appointment to the next, to practices and recitals. And we are busy in mind as we interact with the internet, as the internet entertains us. We scroll through posts on social media, flip through digital pictures of other people's lives, watch children of our friends (and of strangers) grow up across the country, the world even, and comment as if we were there. We send our regards by clicking on a heart. This suffices to keep us connected, I guess, but it lacks so much at the same time. I wonder what we'd do with our time if we didn't have the internet.

You always kept busy. No technology. No internet. You were busy working hard work to make ends meet, to make tomorrow warmer and to fill bellies. I remember how you

7

used to ask me if I was "working hard or hardly working." Yes, you always kept yourself busy working hard. That hard work paid off for your family; they were the why behind your work.

The generation of those who lived, really lived in the heart of the 1900s, less than 100 years ago, are passing away. You are gone, dear Poppa. Your sweetheart lives every day still missing you. She is doing so well, loving her daughter, her grandchildren, and her great-grands, as she calls them. You loved her so. She talks of you often, usually with tears in her eyes and a catch in her voice.

There are so many stories we did not get to talk about while you were here. I am so glad you took the time to write them down. Many who lived through the poverty and frustration of the Great Depression are aging and our chances of hearing them tell their stories are vanishing.

You were a child of the Great Depression. Extended family shared housing, meals, and bridged gaps in paychecks. Your father relied on building bridges, laying rails, and picking cotton. You learned to appreciate the generosity of others. You learned to rely on the simplicity of hard work.

You were born in Texas in 1929, and your true love for over half a century was born in Utah the same year. Your paths crossed twenty years later, but first you had some growing up to do. I wish I had known you then, when you knew you just needed hard work and love to make it last.

I love your story, Poppa. I am so glad you wrote it down.

2 THE BACKSTORY

My grandfather, Charles Lowell McGuire, was born July 2, 1929. Three months later, on October 24, 1929, officially began the Great Depression in the United States of America. That's quite a way to enter life, right into the midst of high unemployment, pervasive poverty, low profits for businesses, and not to mention deflation and the decline of agricultural income. He was just three months old when there was the great Wall Street Crash. That was thousands of miles away in grandiose New York City, New York. It was so many miles away that it may as well have been another continent, except that it wasn't. "The Crash" on Wall Street, as it was later called, affected people in all parts of the country, in the cities and in the farming communities; it didn't matter who you were, the economy pressed in from every side. The McGuires were already poor and things weren't looking up in 1929. The Crash began an economic and social depression never before seen in the United States, but the McGuires rallied, pulled up their boot straps (when they had boots to wear), and held together as family should do when life gives you lemons. They made some sweet, cold lemonade.

The president in office was Franklin D. Roosevelt. He was in the middle of his twelve years as president and just beginning to lead the United States through World War II for the next six years.

That was 1,500 miles away in Washington D.C., so far away on the east coast of this big country. The McGuires were in a little town in the heart of the country called Byers, Texas. Located about 300 miles due north of Austin (the capital of Texas), Byers sits just below the Oklahoma border. It was then and still is today just one square mile wide. A traveler on Texas State Highway 79 might not even know he'd passed through the heart of town. Highway 79 was known as Main Street in Byers, Texas, and connected the larger (though still small) town of Wichita Falls with Interstate 70. In 2010, there were not quite 500 people in

Byers, Texas. Back in 1940, the U.S. Decennial Census documented 427 people in Byers, while in 1929, there wasn't even a census record kept. One more person to add to the population was born in the little town of Byers that year, and he was named Charles Lowell.

3 POPPA WRITES

To put it mildly, the year nineteen hundred and twenty-nine was a bad year. There was already a major depression in full swing across our great nation. When I think back to my youth in Byers, Texas, I cannot in my wildest dreams imagine a worse time or place in history to have been born. I am not complaining. It was to be my first life lesson and this lesson would guide me for the rest of my days.

There would be many times that I would have to pick myself up – sometimes go off in a different direction to bigger and better things. Sometimes it was a wrong direction, and I would go back to where I was and start over again.

My mother, Edna Mae Dunn, a beautiful lady by all accounts, was born in March 1911, and my father, Russell McGuire, was born December 1906. He was a very handsome man, well-respected and liked by everyone, especially Edna Mae. They were married September 4, 1926. Russell was just twenty years old and his blushing bride was a mere fifteen years of age. Without their upbringing, love, support, and example, I could not have accomplished all the things I did in my life. I believe that everything, good and bad, large and small, that a person experiences in his life can affect him for the positive. The good Lord can make positive out of any negative no matter the circumstances.

The night before I was born, there was a big storm brewing in Byers, which was typical for July in north Texas in the middle of what they call "tornado alley." The reason I know it was a strong storm is because everyone went to the storm cellar for the storm to pass and my dad never went to the cellar if there was not a good reason for it. There were high winds, rain, lightning and always the chance of a tornado. That particular night, the storm passed and everyone went back to the house for the rest of the night.

Early the next morning, probably about 4:00 a.m., my mother awoke and decided she had carried me long enough. She had experienced the loss of two babies at birth. First there was Mary Ann, born April 22, 1927, who died due to miscarriage. She was buried at the Byers Riverside Cemetery. And second, Russell Jr. was born March 12, 1928, and died the same day due to inanition. He was probably was buried in their own yard. With the loss of two babies, Mother sure did not want this to happen again.

My mom woke my dad and told him to get Doctor Jones

and her mother as soon as possible. "It's time!" she called out.

Dad sent his older brother, Donald, on his way while my dad stayed with my mom. The rest is history. I was born healthy and strong. Grandmother Dunn was always proud to have been there and to have changed my first diaper. It was July 2, 1929.

On July 4, 1929, when I was just two days old, my dad had the mumps and I had colic, so there was not the usual holiday celebration. I am told my dad carried me on his shoulder all day to keep me from crying.

My Uncle Donald and my Aunt Claudie lived in the same house with my mom and dad. It was called the Glenny house. This house was also the birthplace of my cousin, Don, just three months after me. We were always good friends even though his dad and mine had some terrible fights over the years.

A history of Byers, Texas, by G. C. Boswell, May 1925 states – "The social atmosphere has always been good. There have been very few robberies and burglaries in town and the only murder that has been committed in the town was April 1925, when C. E. Glenny shot and killed his oldest son, Robert." Glenny served ten years in prison then lived a quiet life for the rest of his years in another town. One winter day in old age, he got turned around and headed out of town along a set of railroad tracks. Glenny, disoriented and freezing, died on these tracks and was run over – split in two – by a train some point later. Aside from this murder decades earlier, not much in the way of crimes are mentioned in Clay County history. You will see that this fact speaks mighty well for a town that is twenty-one years old. It was in the Glenny house (where Robert Glenny was murdered) that I was born in four years later.

When I was three months old, and we were still living in the notorious Glenny house, my dad worked on the railroad. One day my mom wanted to see her husband, so she went over to the Red River and proceeded to walk across the mile-long span of the railroad bridge to Oklahoma, one tie at a time, to where my dad was working. When she was about halfway across, she met a train coming straight at us. She was frightened, probably scared to death, but the train slowed and the engineer motioned for her to get down. Bravely she hunched down on the side of the ties with me safely in her arms, and the train actually passed over our heads. We didn't get served the same fate as C. E. Glenny would at the end of his life. Thanks much, Mom.

4 THE 1930S, COTTON PICKING AND OTHER ODD JOBS

My dad had many talents which led to many odd jobs, and he even had his own hamburger stand when he was young in Henrietta. He helped to build and then rebuild the school house in Byers, laying the bricks as a stone mason. He worked on the school as a carpenter in Petrolia. He was an excellent cotton picker, always picking acceptable, clean cotton long before mechanized equipment was built. The trouble with cotton picking by hand is that you could only pick 100 to 150 pounds of cotton, and that's working from dawn to dusk. At 50-cents per 100 pounds, that would only be about $1.00 to $1.50 for a long, hard, day's work. On top of that, the cotton picking season was very short. Dad worked on the Wichita Falls dam project tying steel for a new spillway, although this was only a temporary job. And he worked on the mile-long Red River bridge project, but once it was finished he was out of work.

Dad was an accomplished musician, playing the guitar, violin, and banjo. Although he never played professionally like his brother, Rudy, who aired on the radio in Wichita Falls, my dad played regularly for dances. I remember when I was five years old I would sleep on the stage behind the musicians while Dad played for western dances in Petrolia. All this musical talent apparently never rubbed off on me, though I like to be around good musical talent to this day. Come to find out years later, this talent skipped a generation.

Having all this talent so close to me for twenty years, I was to learn about good workmanship, accuracy, dependability, dedication, honesty, and integrity. All these good traits are not only necessary, they are in fact mandatory in almost anything you want to succeed in. Thanks much, Dad.

Growing up in Byers was difficult to say the least. During the first twelve years of my life, we lived in at least eight different houses, if you can call them houses. Not one of them had running water, electricity, a telephone, a refrigerator, insulation, and none of them had an inside toilet. The outhouse, as we called it, was located about a hundred feet back of the house, and when it was very cold, raining, or the wind was blowing very hard it was a miserable trip.

At the Glenny house where I was born, Mom followed Dad with the mumps and by winter we had moved to a small area above the store owned by my Great-grandfather Dunn and Aunt Bertha. (She wasn't really my aunt, but that's what we called her.)

The house a half block north of Aunt Bertha's was called Liggett house, where my sister, Peggy, was born on August 21, 1932. I was barely two years old, but I still remember lying on the front porch in the shade that summer. It was so hot and humid that I could hardly breathe. I truly thought I would die and it wasn't any better at night.

Our only source of light at night was a kerosene lamp. A small can of kerosene was always kept on the windowsill and one day my curiosity got me in big trouble. I climbed up on the sill and took big a drink from this can of kerosene. Boy did it ever burn going down my throat! To this day I cannot stand the smell of kerosene.

My sister, Martha, was born on May 13, 1935, at the Wilson house. That afternoon Peggy and I were rushed off to the Dunn's house on the hill about one mile west of town. We spent the night there, which was just fine with me, as I got to play with my cousins: Nobie, Haul, Paul, Udell, Faye, and Rufus. I now understand why we never before and never since spent the night at the Dunn's place – just too many kids for one small house on a hill.

That night at the Dunn's place I had to sleep between my twin cousins, Haul and Paul, who were two years older than I was. What an awful night – I thought I would suffocate! After we had all gone to bed, my grandfather got down on his knees by his bed and prayed quite loudly, in fact loud enough for everyone to hear clearly. I guess a little dose of religion each night wouldn't hurt anyone.

Sometime during the night, I felt my cousins shifting about in the bed. I tried to ignore them and go back to sleep, but once they were awake, so was I. We three went out to the front porch to relieve ourselves. Of course then there was a contest to see who could urinate the farthest from the front porch, maybe even hit the fence which was several yards away. There was a full moon that night and it was almost as light as day. Paul won that contest and earned bragging rights for days.

Peggy and I were taken back to our house the next day and we had a new little sister, Martha, named after Grandmother Dunn. Grandmother was thrilled to have her name passed on to her granddaughter. We were simply told the stork brought Martha. I guess we never thought to ask for details and we were none the wiser. Martha was here, and now we were a family of five.

5 A CHRISTMAS MIRACLE AND A HARD WINTER IN THE WILSON HOUSE

We lived in the Wilson house for two and a half years, probably longer than any other place in Byers. Christmas came and went and was usually pretty bleak for us. One year Uncle Lindol and Aunt Lennie came from Wichita Falls and brought me a little cast iron fire engine and I believe "Santa" brought me a little red wagon. I was told later my grandfather had paid for most of the cost of the little red wagon. This was the best Christmas I can remember in Byers.

Things were quite depressing for us the last Christmas we

spent at the Wilson house. In addition to it being very cold, there was snow with long icicles hanging down from the front porch and the big disappointment was Santa didn't come. No gifts! No Christmas tree! No turkey dinner! I am sure my mom and dad felt much worse than we three kids felt.

We went out into the cold to play. It was very cold, although probably not much colder than it was in the house. We had no wood to make a fire and, like most houses those days, the house was not insulated.

We didn't stay outside very long. Not because of the cold, miserable weather though. We came running back with a beautiful Christmas tree! We found it in back of our house by the alley. Mr. and Mrs. Christian, who owned one of the two small grocery stores in town, lived behind us and we think they tossed the tree in the alley. We were so excited, thinking there was a Santa after all.

In January things did not get any better. It was a cold month with drizzle that made it especially miserable. Looking back some sixty years later, it was just another straw that broke the camel's back, as they say. Even though dad worked hard, things just did not get any better. We couldn't seem to catch a break.

We were out of firewood and so very cold. Dad did not like to ask for help, but he finally relented. He and I walked to Grandfather Dunn's place to borrow a wagon and two horses to pull the wagon. I was maybe seven or eight years old, and here I was learning another life lesson about survival. There were many more lessons to learn just over the horizon.

We were headed toward town, one mile, then headed north and down Parker Hill. Here we were able to find wood down near the Big Wichita River. Dad cut wood and I loaded it onto the wagon. He was an experienced wood cutter. I had so much to learn from him. I watched him cut the wood, knowing someday he'd let me fetch the wood for our family. I wanted to be helpful.

Dad took the horses and wagon back to Grandfather by himself, as I was just too exhausted, wet, and cold to go with him. This day will always be etched in my memory, and a good feeling always comes over me when I think about it. We had wood now, but still no food in the house, so Mom scraped together the ingredients to make some hot bread. We had a little butter she had gotten from the Dunns, so when dad came home from returning the wagon, we had hot bread and butter. It was so good I remember shaking uncontrollably as I sat on the bench eating the hot bread. We didn't even wait for it to cool to cut it. It was the best thing I had ever tasted.

One day during the cold weather, there was snow and icicles. They called it a "Texas Norther." We put on all the layers of clothes that we had and headed out to walk to the Dunn's house to get a meal, as things were not getting any better.

Our neighbors, Mr. and Mrs. Smyers, were well aware of the dire conditions at our house. Their house was the next house just north of us, and Mrs. Smyers would use my mom now and then to clean her beautiful two-story home. Sometimes I would work for her, too – weeding or cleaning – and she would always sit me down and feed me before I went home. She knew I was hungry.

This cold day we were walking to the Dunn's house, Mr. Smyers came out and told my dad there was some food stuff available in Henrietta, the county seat of Clay County. Of course we had no car, so Mr. Smyers took him to Henrietta in his pickup truck. Now we had food: welfare food. There were dry beans, rice, flour, sugar, oatmeal, and some powdered milk. Even to this day I love the flavor of powdered milk.

Late one afternoon, almost dark, there was a storm brewing. Dad, as always, had his eye on this storm and as the wind hit extremely hard and the lightning strikes were close together, he took me to the cellar door back of the house, raised the door and ran back to get my mom and two sisters.

With everyone inside (or so he thought), he slammed the cellar door and tied it down with wire to keep the high winds from ripping it off the hinges when he suddenly realized, *Lowell is not here!* He was panic-stricken, *No Lowell!* He untied the door and rushed out into the storm to look for me. The lightning strikes were all around him and he could not see me, even when the sky was lit up like daytime with lightning.

He ran out front to the road and when the lightning would strike, he would look to the north toward town and then to the south toward Byers Lake. *Still no Lowell!* He ran past the open cellar door to the alley again, looking north and south. *No Lowell!* Then another lightning strike and there I was almost to town and still going. He ran and caught me, picked me up and ran all the way back to safety of the cellar. I had gone for a late night stroll, walking in my sleep. My dad said, "This boy needs some watching!"

Soon we were to move again. I can only guess that with my dad unable to get work, we could not afford the five dollars per month for rent. Property owners would let us stay in their house rent free if my dad was not working until they had a renter who could pay, and then we would be asked to move.

Aunt Dimple, my dad's half-sister, and her husband came to visit us one day and took me fishing in the Little Wichita River. This was very exciting for me and little did I know then that we would one day go fishing again together in

California.

On the river bank I found a fishing rod and reel in the weeds. It was a great day. Aunt Dimple and I remained close for many decades to come.

6 POPPA'S WORLD

My grandfather's stories live on in the words he penned and the stories he told me in my youth: I can see him cutting wood with his dad, sleep-walking toward town during the storm, and fishing along the riverbank with Aunt Dimple. He grew up in a very different time, and his stories give me a taste of his world — a world I've never seen except in my mind. I've been to Texas only once a long time ago for a basketball tournament. The expanse that is Texas is mind-boggling. The hot summers and cold winters are not where I'd like to grow up without air conditioning and a furnace. Sometimes my kids ask about my Poppa. I tell them about a kid named Lowell who grew up barefoot and on dirt roads in Texas. I tell them a story like this:

Lowell worked in the cotton fields before school and often again after school. He didn't check in often at home. No one expected him home until dinnertime or after. He was eager to get to work, up before his siblings and out the door often without breakfast. His legs were tan from the hot, Texas, summer sun. His feet were calloused from dirt paths and back roads. And his mind was always set on working.

Sometimes Lowell went without shoes, because he had only one pair that was falling apart and didn't really fit anyway. He didn't seem to mind, even when the other school kids made comments in the yard or gave him sideways glances as he slid into his seat in the school room just in the nick of time. Sure, he needed to bathe more frequently, but he was hard to nail down long enough to get him in the tub. He was stinky, there's no denying that fact. And if Edna Mae caught a good whiff of him, she told him, "Git in that tub or else, mister." Lowell always said that he'd take a dip in the lake to clean off. That'd be good enough.

It wasn't far to the lake. A few miles south was all, and a few miles was nothing to a kid who walked everywhere if he didn't currently have a bicycle to ride. But a few miles in a storm, or the stifling humidity of a summer day, made a few miles seems that much farther.

Lake Wichita was man-made in 1901, desperately needed for irrigation of fields. Plantations aside, hot summers in Texas call for swimming in a lake. And that's just what Lake Wichita was good for. Located three miles south of Wichita Falls proper and over 2,200 acres on a map, the lake was designed by businessman Joseph A. Kemp and his brother-in-law, Frank Kell. Both men were considered to be founders of Wichita Falls in the early 1900s. Kemp served as the county treasurer of Wichita County in the late 1890s.

Wichita River spanned two counties and Kemp proposed that the lake could be dammed and a reservoir built to help with irrigation of the dry Texas deserts. Issue arose when the Texas Constitution of 1876 forbade the use of bonds for the building of dams for the use of irrigation. Kemp didn't give up and he created the private Lake Wichita Irrigation and Water Company. He knew full well that water is worth its weight in gold in a desert land.

As luck would have it, a heavy rain caused nearby Holliday Creek to overflow into a basin and Kemp capitalized on nature's good providence. This site would be the new location for Kemp's soon-to-be Lake Wichita. By the turn of the century, the lake's bottom had been dredged to the tune of $175,000. This was no small sum just before the turn of the twentieth century.

The city government tried to turn Lake Wichita into a tourist destination, first establishing a municipal electric trolley, but by 1912 the lakefront property was sold to private businesses. The city bought the property back in 1920 and set up annual carnivals to bring in tourists. This event lasted for a while, but eventually tourism dwindled, and the carnivals moved on.

Twenty years later, the carnivals at the lake weren't as popular, and Lowell may have taken baths in this same lake. Or he did when he could take time off work, school, and chores. He rarely felt like being lazy, but sometimes the stink even got the best of him. It was probably then that you could find Lowell bathing at the lake in hot, summer months.

The fourth of July is special in all parts of the United States, no matter where you live or how much money you have to celebrate. Setting off fireworks is just what boys do on the Independence Day. Lowell spent time with his cousins, Haul, Paul and Udell, whenever he could, and these boys were a bit older and always a little intimidating. They'd come over to see who they could scare and maybe even impress with their fireworks and jumbo firecrackers. When Haul, Paul, and Udell left to head home, Lowell followed. He felt like one of the big boys. Soon enough, it was Lowell's turn to light a jumbo firecracker.

Scared to death, but emboldened to bravery, Lowell nodded and took the firecracker. They'd shown him how to light the firecracker and throw it before it exploded in his hand. He lit the firecracker and tossed it to the ground about ten feet away.

Nothing.

The firecracker didn't explode. No big bang. No burst of smoke. Lowell didn't know what he'd done wrong. He carefully went over and picked it up. Upon inspection, it looked fine and reminded him of how his dad smoked a cigarette every now and then. He tentatively put the firecracker between his lips, like he'd seen his dad do, and sucked.

Bang!

Big mistake. The loud explosion almost burst his eardrums and the pain! Oh the tremendous pain! His lips were burnt beyond recognition. And he knew he'd be in serious trouble when he got home.

He turned tail and ran home, laughter following him as the big boys relished the idiocy of their little cousin. All the way home without stopping he ran, right into the back door and slammed the screen.

His mom was standing at the kitchen table and Lowell came to a halt. He raised his gaze to meet hers, scared of what she'd say and more of what she'd do when she found out what he'd done.

The biggest grin spread over his mom's face and she started laughing so hard that she doubled over, hands on the table next to the bowl of potatoes she'd been peeling. She shook her head and put her arm around little Lowell. For days, every time she looked at her son, she couldn't help but laughing at the natural consequences of a little mischief and a lot of dumb luck.

7 DUCK FOR LUNCH, SQUIRREL FOR DINNER

For the rest of my life I have had a healthy respect for fireworks, any fireworks. I like them as far away as possible.

My dad had a pretty good job for the times, working on the Wichita Falls dam and spillway project. We were even able to have a car of our own. It was a four-door, black, 1934 Plymouth. This was the first car I remember having in our family, although it wasn't ours for very long. Soon, when the Wichita Falls dam job ran out, there would be no more house, no more car, and no more food on the table.

Cotton picking time was almost upon us. Cotton was planted around Good Friday of Easter week. Some said cotton should be planted under a full moon. The cotton was harvested three months later. This meant the "ginning season," as they called it, was July, August, and September – the hottest months of the year in the dust bowl of Texas. Cotton production depended on rain and sun. Cotton picking depended on many workers. Those were long, back-breaking days of work.

One wagon filled with cotton makes just one bale of cotton. It took one whole acre of a cotton field to fill a wagon to 1,500 pounds, then it was taken to the gin.

My dad was a reputable man, liked and respected by everyone in and around Byers. He was able to get us a small two-room house on the Langford ranch northeast of Byers a few miles, so we could pick cotton for the Langford family.

My mom and dad picked cotton all day from dawn till dusk with us kids just hanging out or playing in the shade under the wagon used to haul the cotton to the cotton gin. It was long days for everyone. The Dunns would drive down with my grandad, Udell, Faye, Haul and Paul to pick cotton with us.

Soon my Grandmother Burch and Aunt Dimple came down from Wichita Falls to pick cotton with us, too. They stayed with us in our small house and each day Grandmother Burch was up exercising before she went out to pick cotton. I learned another life lesson from my Grandmother Burch – to this day I exercise every morning.

While we worked in the cotton patch, my dad found time to take his shot gun and take me with him a short distance to some small lakes and shoot ducks to help feed our hungry group. Once there were so many ducks, he actually got three with one shot. That's how I remember it, at least.

My dad was a man of many talents.

While on the Langford ranch my dad bought a used car. We needed it so we could get to town to buy some food. Once I went with him and on the way home he drove at what I thought was supersonic speed, which was maybe fifty miles per hour. Wow! About a mile from home the axle broke on the car. Again we were without wheels.

Nothing new for us, I guess.

When cotton season was over there was no work for my dad so we had to leave the Langford's house. With no money built up from the seasonal work and no place to live, we moved to the bottom land on the Dunn's ranch on the Big Wichita River.

We lived in a small shed for many months in the fall of 1937. My dad cut many cords of wood for the Dunns. I am sure this was to pay our rent. He fed his family trapping ducks, quail, and rabbits. One day he took me down to the river. Using grasshoppers and worms for bait, he set out a trout line to catch fish, again to feed the family. The next morning we came back and had five catfish.

While we could not afford many .22 shot shells for our borrowed .22 rifle, one day we had surprise company and we needed meat for the table. It was Sunday and they just drove up. Dad took the rifle and hurried out. A short time later, he came back with two squirrels and we had them for dinner. Squirrel is delicious, especially when you're hungry and the food is hot.

When we lived on the river, the old shed we lived in had a corrugated steel roof. One day when a storm came with hail bigger than golf balls, the noise was so loud you could not talk to anyone. Dad said he couldn't even hear himself think.

Going without shoes all summer you had real tough soles on your feet but not tough enough for cockleburs. We had a solid patch of these stickers about a hundred feet across that we had to walk through when we hiked to the Dunn's house. I devised a way to get to the Dunn's house while minimizing the pain: Run as fast as you can until you get across, and then sit down and pick out the stickers. I called that good ol' American ingenuity. (Actually, I stole this idea from Paul.)

The winter of 1937, we moved to another house about three blocks from town across the street from where Martha was born. It was a two-room house and it was better for my Dad to be close to town if he was needed for work.

Mrs. Christian again was our good neighbor, only one block away. She invited us to join them in their storm cellar when necessary. Soon a serious storm came in the form of high winds, rain, and hail, so we went down and spent a few hours in their very nice cement storm cellar. When we returned home we found our house had been moved several feet. The whole house up and moved! Otherwise it was not damaged. Again, another life lesson for me: I now had a real respect for the power of Mother Nature.

I guess you could say we did not miss the things we did not have. We carried all our water from a well across the street. With no electricity we had no refrigerator, only an ice box and we could not afford any ice to put in it to keep it cold, so we could not store any food in it. It was an empty box most of the time.

One very hot summer day, when I was ten years old, my mom sent me to town to get a nickel's worth of ice. Five cents would buy about ten pounds of ice. Mom wanted to make some iced tea. This would be a real summertime treat for us. She gave me a nickel and off I went to town running all the way with this nickel held tightly in my hand. I was barefoot. After I purchased the ice, I ran for home. It was not so easy to run with ten pounds of ice and the hot ground seemed to get hotter by the minute. At one point, about half way home I just could not stand the heat on my feet any longer so I sat down in the shade of a telephone pole and put my feet on the block of ice. Only then could I continue my journey home. The prize, of course, was a big glass of mom's delicious iced tea after the dirt had been rinsed off the ice.

8 TO THE PROMISED LAND

It wasn't a last straw, but a continuation of last straws. My mom and dad had given their all to try to make things work in Byers.

It wasn't that there was never any work in Byers. It was that it was always seasonal or temporary. When the crops were being harvested (cotton, corn or wheat), there were good but temporary jobs. Other jobs like building a spillway for a dam or working on a bridge in West Texas or the mile long bridge across the Red River meant there was work until the work was done. It was those days we had food on our table and a roof over our heads.

We still could not afford the five dollars per month rent. The winter of 1940 was a bad one. I think my dad, remembering when he had accepted the only welfare in his life and how badly he had felt about this, was determined that it would not happen again.

The year was 1941, a momentous time for our country and our family, as there were clouds of war on the horizon and things were so bad I did not even have shoes to wear to school that year. It was the month of May that my dad announced that he was going to California. He had heard they had work there and he had been offered a ride from a long-time friend. Within days my dad was gone and we were alone. Mom was beside herself but knew she couldn't let the family fall apart in his absence.

About two months passed and we received a letter from my dad in California. It was simple and to the point: "Sell or give away everything we own, even if you can get only fifty cents for it, and get a ride to California." My dad had found a good permanent job. We did not know at the time but there was a much better life waiting for us in California. My dad was never out of work until he retired. My mom would work for Los Angeles County for thirty years before she retired. It was the only real job she ever had.

The preacher in my grandfather's church, along with his wife and two teenage children and the four of us McGuires would make the 1,450 mile journey from Texas to California in a new 1941 Studebaker American car. It was a stressful trip to say the least. Before we left, my grandfather took us to Fort Worth, Texas and I had my first store-bought haircut before our big adventure across the United States. This was the first of many "firsts."

Fraught with many unknowns, our trip from Byers, Texas to California was long, hot, and uncomfortable. There were no air conditioners, only a window air conditioner that needed a continuous supply of water and cooled by evaporation. You can imagine how sweaty and sticky we were in that Studebaker!

When we went through Needles, California and crossed the Colorado River, we were in awe of the size of this river and the beautiful clear, clean water it carried. It was nothing like any river we had ever seen in Texas as our rivers were forever the color of clay. Our spirits were lifted, even though it was 135 degrees that day in the desert.

We arrived in Downey, California the first week of July in 1941. I celebrated turning twelve with fresh ocean air and blue skies. Everything was green and beautiful with orange groves everywhere and every home had a lawn. What a difference from where we had come! It was cool all the time and only twelve miles to the ocean. We stopped at the ice house and were given directions to where my uncle and cousins lived. My grandmother lived behind their home on the next street, and my Aunt Dimple and Uncle Jack lived about one block away. We had a joyous family reunion. Soon we made a short trip over to Bellflower to see something I had never seen before: a supermarket. We took a trunk full of food home with us. We were now truly rich!

Within a few days we moved into our first home in California, an apartment on the next street over from my uncle's house. I couldn't believe my eyes when I saw that this house had an inside toilet, a refrigerator, and two bedrooms. It was huge! It was a mansion compared to our homes in the past.

Dad took us all to a movie at the local theater. Our lives were surely changing for the better. I thought I was dreaming.

Growing up in the middle of the country, I had never seen the ocean. I didn't even know what to dream the ocean might look like. One Sunday we took a drive down Cherry Avenue over Signal Hill to Ocean Avenue to a small park in Long Beach. We walked down some stairs and under Ocean Avenue to see the Pacific Ocean for the first time. I will never forget the awesome sight that was before us. It was so big with the huge waves pounding the shoreline. The vast ocean rolled before me. The power of the waves was almost incomprehensible. What an amazing creation. Surely there must be an amazing Creator.

There were paved roads everywhere and tall palm trees lined both sides of the boulevard as far as the eye could see. We had surely arrived in the land of plenty and this land was to be exceptionally good to me.

In California we were able to pay our rent each month, buy enough food at the supermarket to adequately feed our family, and I never went without shoes again. These were all more "firsts" in my book.

Within a few weeks I was to start at the local junior high school, but when we moved to another house just two weeks later, it was necessary to change schools. I suppose we were used to moving by this time. I started school in the seventh grade. Soon I realized either all the California kids would have to get used to my thick Texas drawl or I had to make a quick change. After at least five fights in just the first week, I relented and I swear I lost my southern accent over one weekend. I guess the old saying is true: "When in Rome, do as the Romans."

It proved to be a good move on my part, and as time went by I developed a group of about eight friends who hung out together, played handball, and had swim class together. We kept in touch for more than fifty years.

We were in California only about five months, when on December 7, 1941, our country was attacked by the Japanese at Pearl Harbor and the United States joined the

Allies in World War II. All homes were ordered completely blacked out so no light could be seen from the outside. All street lights, traffic lights, and neon lights were turned off so enemy planes could not navigate using these lights. We had an air raid warden for every block that would inspect houses to be sure there were no violations. Cars drove without lights.

One night all the sirens in Downey sounded and we had anti-aircraft guns firing at what appeared to be enemy aircraft in the sky above Downey. I remember my dad pulling back the drapes and looking out toward the city of Downey as I looked over his shoulder. We knew something was going on as we could hear all this noise coming from anti-aircraft gun emplacements that were located all over the city of Downey. Tracer shells lit up their path and they appeared to come straight at us and went just over our second story house. This was very frightening and I will not forget this as long as I live. The only damage, except to our nerves, was an oil well near Santa Barbara that got hit by gun fire from a submarine.

Soon we moved to 310 Conrad Street, another rental unit. By the time I was fourteen years old, I was working steadily for our landlord, Mr. Hocker, irrigating the fields, driving the farm equipment, trucks, tractors, and soon his beautiful 1936 Pontiac sedan all over the country with him always by my side. Mr. Hocker was a good driver but he had a huge belly and was very uncomfortable behind the wheel. What a great opportunity for me.

One day I was driving one of his trucks down the road as Mr. Hocker drove along behind me. A patrolman stopped me right there on Paramount Boulevard. Mr. Hocker talked the policeman into writing the ticket out for him (and not for me, the underage driver) and he went to see Judge Boone in Downey. I never heard any more about the ticket. Each time we went out driving, Mr. Hocker always bought us a Hines root beer. This was a major treat in those days!

I would sometimes work all day on Saturdays, a full twelve hours, irrigating Mr. Hocker's farm, driving his big truck, spreading cow manure in orange orchards, or hauling trash out of someone's back yard. He taught me how to work and he expected a lot out of me even though I was only fourteen years old at the time. The pay was not much but it was not a big concern – I had a job and was enjoying every minute of it. There was always one rule Mr. Hocker had for me: Attend the Nazarene Church every Sunday.

By the time I was fifteen, I had my own bicycle, but my dad would not allow me to ride it on the streets until I was sixteen. I always thought this went back to my sleep-walking episode when I was seven years old in Byers. I guess my dad had decided I still needed some watching to keep me out of trouble.

By 1945, I was working the supermarkets in Downey as a

box boy, stocker, delivery man, and once as a cook in the deli department at a local grocery store. My job at the deli was to arrive early, make the barbecue sauce from scratch and barbecue the ribs to sell hot over the counter all day. The manager told me that the smell of those ribs surely increased sales all over the store.

I was now sixteen years old and allowed to ride my bike on the streets of Downey. I could work until 9:00pm and get home safely, my dad figured. When I had a Sunday off, I usually went on a bike trip with my cousin Don.

I learned to ride my bike everywhere. I wanted to explore this new land. A challenging ride was a twelve-mile trip to Long Beach over Signal Hill. We would usually leave early and get there before any of the rides opened. The roller coaster, Ferris wheel and other attractions sat still and quiet in the early morning. We would ride around the Pike in Long Beach and Rainbow Pier and head for home. This was all well and good as we had no money to spend anyway. All this was a real thrill for a country boy who only a couple years prior not only did not have a bike, but did not even have a pair of shoes to start school.

By early 1946, my cousin Don was working at Rockview Dairy Farms and he told me I probably could get a job there. Little did either of us know that I would spend most of my working life in the milk business.

A lesson I learned from my mother was always keeping something on "lay-away" at the stores. I would pay a little on them each time I got a pay check, maybe 10- or 25-cents at a time. I enjoyed giving my parents gifts, so I put a $54.00 Bulova watch on lay-away at the local jeweler's store. When I made the last payment, I gave it to my mom. She was so happy to get such a nice gift and I had that wonderful feeling giving it to her. That watch cost a lot of money in those days. I also bought her a new Maytag

Dutch oven stove and she always had hot food for me when I came home from work late at night.

I found a beautiful D18 Martin guitar at a music store where I took music lessons on a steel guitar. After many months of small payments, I paid it off and surprised my dad with this gift. He enjoyed it for about twenty-three years when one day he called me and insisted I come over at once so he could gift the guitar to my oldest daughter.

It was about this time that I was offered an opportunity to help my folks buy a new home in Downey. I borrowed $1000, which was 10% of the total cost of the new home. The subject was never brought up again and my mom and dad had the beautiful home they never dreamed they would own. Dad always took great pride in taking care of the house and yard. Mom took care of the inside, furnishing it properly, one piece of furniture at a time, and showing everyone how proud she was to have her own house.

Once I got my driver's license, I bought a Model A Ford from my dad for $125 to drive to school. Boy, was that a special day! He believed I should pay my own way and I have always had a good feeling when I bought something for myself. I drove this car while I was in high school and was known as the best Model A driver in Downey. I survived some really close calls and I believe learned some life lessons along the way.

I graduated from Downey High School in 1947, achieving something my mom and dad were never able to do. It was because of their persistence and hard work that I was able to accomplish this great feat for a boy who grew up in the little town of Byers, Texas.

9 LOVE AND MARRIAGE GO TOGETHER

"Like a horse and carriage," or so they say. I never had a horse. Never wanted one. I consider all of my life, the ups and downs, the good times and the bad, very exciting with always something to look forward to in a positive way. Even the hard work, long hours, sometimes two and three jobs at a time, created a challenge each day of my life. The high point, over and above everything else has to be the year 1949.

A beautiful Utah girl showed up in the neighborhood visiting her brother. Her name was Margaret, and she was without a doubt the most beautiful girl I had ever seen and soon we were going to church together in Downey with my sisters, Peggy and Martha.

Margaret and I started dating, going to the theatre, miniature golf, the drive-in diner, and the county fair. I still remember the first time I kissed her. I parked in her brother's driveway after a date, opened her door to let her out of the car, took her hand and we went for a walk around the block. We stopped on the corner and I kissed her the first time, partly missing her lips and getting lipstick all over my face. I can still see her laughing with her beautiful, smiling eyes.

It was surely love at first sight for me. When she received a big bouquet of red roses from an admirer in Utah, I knew I must act fast.

Only about six weeks after Margaret arrived in California from Utah, we were driving home from the diner when I stopped the car at the corner and asked her what she was doing on Sunday. Margaret said, "I don't know of anything."

It was then I asked her, "Would you like to get married on Sunday?"

After a long thoughtful silence – it seemed like an eternity – she said "Yes." I kissed her and got it right this time and took her home and parked in her driveway. Before I opened the door to let her out, she turned and asked, "How will we get by?"

I looked Margaret in the eyes and said, "We can make it only if we work together as a team."

Everyone was asleep when I came home so there was no one to tell the exciting news. I laid awake almost all night thinking about everything that needed to be done before Sunday. This was already Tuesday night. I must have fallen asleep and slept long, because Mom and Dad were already gone to work the next morning when I awoke. When I returned home at 7:00pm, 1 was so anxious to tell them that I blurted it out all at once – "Mom? Dad? Would you like to come to my wedding on Sunday?"

This was Wednesday night. Talk about short notice! Once again total silence. Twice in just two days. My Dad picked up his guitar, and started to play and sing this song:

I want a girl,

Just like the girl that married dear ol' dad.

A good ol' fashioned girl with love so true.

His tears flowed freely. I trust they were tears of joy.

Margaret called her dad in Utah and told him of her plans to get married on Sunday. Understand now that this was Thursday. He said, "I hope you know what you are doing," and added, "It won't last till spring." He informed her that he would promptly take her off his accounts, if she was to be a married woman. She was fine with that, and fifty-three years later, we are still trying to determine which spring he was talking about.

I worked six ten-hour days and my pay at Shelter Superior Dairy was $260 per month. The monthly car payment was $110. That left us with $150 for the rest of our needs. There would be some tough times ahead, but we had each other, and that was enough.

We went down to the Nazarene Church in Downey, talked to the reverend and decided on a small ceremony at the parsonage on Fifth Street. We went to Long Beach to get our marriage license and after our blood test, we were ready to get married.

Next we found a small but lovely furnished apartment. All we had to do was move in our clothes. We were ready for the big day.

November 20th, 1949, I awoke early and more than a little nervous. I can't believe that with all my nerves, I shaved that morning with an old fashioned straight razor and didn't cut myself. That would be the last time I would use a straight razor, just too dangerous for a boy, now a man, with all this responsibility.

Off I went to the parsonage to meet Margaret and get married for the first and only time. My Dad had told me once, "Marriage is forever, so there can be no second time!"

Only close friends and relatives were invited as we wanted a small private ceremony. I had not seen the bride all morning because of an old tradition – and then there she was, pretty as a picture, even more beautiful than I had remembered the day before. We said our "I dos" and I got to kiss the bride. I made sure to get it right this time!

In all honesty, I really did not know Margaret very well, as I had met her only about eight weeks prior and she didn't know me very well. As we drove to our wedding celebration at my parents' house, Margaret was probably as nervous as me. She took this moment to tell me that she was not a very good cook, as her mother had always done all the cooking at home – as if whether or not she was a good cook would make any difference.

We were in front of a corner market, so I turned into the parking lot and told Margaret I would be right back. I came back and presented her with a brand new can opener and said, "At least we won't starve to death." We both laughed for years when we used that can opener in our kitchen.

Margaret turned out to be a great cook. When I came home from work each night, there was always a hot, delicious meal on the table. Margaret always kept our beautiful, tiny apartment spick and span.

10 A FATEFUL CHANGE

About October 1950, I made a fateful decision to leave Shelter Superior Dairy. I needed to make more money and thought it would be best to get out of production and try my hand at sales. Creamery work was long hours and I was always wet and getting cut on glass from broken milk bottles.

An independent distributor had noticed that I had good work habits and considered me to be honest. He offered me a sales job making more money and it appeared easier – not as time-consuming as washing milk bottles ten hours each day. Margaret and I discussed this proposed change and decided to try a new profession.

On my milk delivery route I always knocked on a few extra doors each day to get new customers and build up the volume of my sales. Getting used to working with the public was a challenge for me although I was making steady progress. The more sales I had meant more money on my paycheck.

The morning of January 21, 1951, a car collided with the right rear wheel of my milk delivery truck causing it to crash onto its left side. Later police estimated the car was going fifty-five miles per hour in a twenty-five miles per hour residential zone. I fell out the open door of my milk truck, as there were no safety belts in those days, and I called out for God to save me!

I did not know at the time that I would "almost not make it." I hit the blacktop on the left side of my face and the truck landed on top of me. According to witnesses, the truck bounced one time before coming to rest on my shoulders. I was pinned to the blacktop. I could not breathe with all this weight on my shoulders. My pelvis was fractured and I was unconscious.

It was a miracle my skull was not fractured when I hit the pavement. A second miracle was that the truck did not sever my spinal cord as it crushed me.

That day I saw the hand of God. Four angels arrived: each on a specific mission, each on a specific schedule. Each angel completed his or her mission and then was gone.

With my shoulders pinned to the ground, I was lying on the pavement unconscious and not breathing. Bystanders later told me that an old lumber truck came slowly around the corner. Witnesses said the driver appeared to be on a mission, and the timing was remarkable! He had not seen the accident. He had just arrived at the precise time, not too early, not too late. He would assist in saving my life. Very calmly, I am told, with bystanders telling him it was too late and that I was already dead, he tied a very large, old, frayed rope to my milk truck and pulled it upright with his lumber truck. His job was done and he was gone.

The milk truck was no longer on top of me, but I was still not breathing. My air passages had filled with blood and congealed to a solid state. Along came another angel, again with remarkable timing. I had just been talking with this lady who was standing in front of my customer's house. I found out later that this special lady had first aid training during World War II when she was an air raid warden. She opened up my air passage by putting her hand down my throat and soon I began to breathe again. Her part in saving my life was done and she was gone. Just another coincidence? I think not!

As I lay there before the ambulance came, two young men who were visiting on the corner where the accident occurred gave me encouragement, telling me I was going to be alright, that I was going to make it. I call these young men angels #3 and #4. God's timing? I think so. And then they were gone.

Soon the ambulance arrived, only a few minutes passed I am sure, even though it seemed like an awful long time. As I was loaded onto the stretcher to be transported to the hospital, I told the ambulance attendants to "tell my wife that I love her." I was taken to Women's and Children's

Hospital on Long Beach Boulevard in Lynwood, as it was very close to the scene of the accident. They wanted to stabilize me for the trip to Long Beach Community Hospital.

Since we had no phone in our home, personnel from the hospital called our landlady, Mrs. Dean. She went straight to get Margaret to take her to the hospital. Mrs. Dean told Margaret that I had been hurt in a very bad accident, and gave her a stern lecture: "Do not break down and cry in front of Lowell."

After the doctor briefed Margaret on my condition, it was time to transfer me to Long Beach Community Hospital for treatment. The ambulance had waited so I could be transported as soon as possible. The driver of the ambulance was able to deliver my message to Margaret. She rode in the ambulance with me and held my hand all the way. I was beginning to think that I might make it.

I was to spend seven long weeks in the hospital with Margaret coming to see me every day. Each day I was taken to the physical therapy department in the basement of the hospital for treatment. I was not making much progress so one day they put me alongside a twelve year old boy with polio. Even though his limbs were quite deformed due to the advanced stages of the disease, he was churning out the exercises like a machine, as he was instructed. It did not take long till I realized I had been set up. If he could do all these exercises with his major disabilities, 1 could do it too. I was on my way to recovery, maybe not one hundred percent, but close to it.

One day Margaret came to visit me and walked up to the left side of my bed and stood there for a very long time. Even though my eyes were open I had not seen her. Suddenly I realized I had lost almost all my vision in the left side of both eyes due to bleeding in the back right side of my brain. This was confirmed by tests and my vision has not changed in all these years. I had to learn how to get along with this vision deficiency.

Margaret came on the bus to visit me each day about noon. She'd stay until my folks came to visit about five, and then she went home with them. This was a long day for her for seven weeks, but she did not ever miss a day. This helped me recuperate much sooner, I am sure!

I was off work for a full year due to my injuries, and receiving only $50 weekly from workman's compensation. Our landlords, Mr. and Mrs. John Dean, saved us during this very rough time. Mrs. Dean asked what we planned to do while I recovered from my injuries. Margaret told her we supposed we would have to move in with my folks in Downey. Mrs. Dean shook her head and said we could stay in our apartment if we wished. "If you can never pay us," she said, "that will be just fine with us." She smiled. "Lowell will need a lot of peace and quiet to recover from his injuries."

One day the I.R.S. came by to find out why I had not paid my taxes for 1950. Mrs. Dean usually questioned everyone who came to see us, so I could rest and heal, and the I.R.S. was no exception. She finally relented and let him in. After seeing me in my condition, he decided he could not get blood out of a turnip, as they say, so he went away and never came back. Mr. and Mrs. Dean were truly great people.

About the middle of December 1951, we received our settlement check from the insurance company. It would not be much by today's standards, but it was a great feeling to be able to pay our bills and we thought we had hit the jackpot. Our attorney had been paying our car payment so we settled up with him, paying him twenty-five percent of our settlement for handling our case for one year.

The first stop was to repay the Deans for back rent for a full year and thank them from the bottom of our hearts. What a wonderful feeling to have survived the past year, be out of debt, and be able to plan for the future! Most of all, I was just glad to be alive.

11 BABY DAYS AND DREAMS OF THOUSANDS OF GALLONS OF MILK

We bought our first home in Whittier in January 1952. We thought we had arrived, but there were still a lot of unknowns out there. I had no job, and did not know if anyone would hire me after what I had been through the past year. A friend of my uncle called and offered me a job installing walk-in refrigerators all around the country. I took the job.

I remember my first day on the job was installing a large walk-in refrigerator in a small supermarket on a huge cattle ranch. The location was a hundred miles out in the desert. We drove out early in order to arrive by 7:00am. Breakfast was being served in the bunkhouse for all the cowboys, and we were told to help ourselves. I still remember the huge pans of bacon cooking in the oven with biscuits and scrambled eggs. I ate until I couldn't eat another bite. I'll never forget that breakfast.

We were on the clock working for twenty-four hours until the job was done. When one of us got so tired and could not go on, we just laid down on the floor and took a short snooze, then it was back to work. I was so happy about being back to work, any work, I was overcome by a feeling of thankfulness and unexplained energy. I realized from this experience that I could work very long hours and survive. This was to become my method of operation for many years to come.

While I liked the job at Custom Refrigeration, I knew something was missing. I needed to do some searching to find out what it was. I went to work with my dad at Union

Steel as an expediter. This job was challenging, but very boring. I had no sense of accomplishment. After a tragic turn of events and a death in my extended family, I quit my steel job.

Of course, as fate would have it, Margaret was pregnant now with our first daughter and I needed a paycheck. I worked for a company making rockets, but this wasn't fulfilling. I think I had milk in my veins and needed to get back into the dairy business.

Soon I found a job about a block down the street at Washington Dairy in Whittier. I found myself washing bottles and milk tanks, wet all the time and happy. I was back where I belonged and it would pay off one day. I just knew it.

I found a job at Foremost Dairy in Los Angeles on swing shift so I could work the morning shift at Washington Dairy and the swing shift at Foremost. I found I was testing my limits, most days working sixteen hours and sometimes I would find myself falling asleep at noon as I drove the Santa Ana freeway going from Whittier to Los Angeles.

At Foremost Dairy it was my job to wash the big milk tanks. I could wash all my fourteen tanks in four hours or less. I would take a shower, put on a clean, dry white uniform, and shadow the foreman for the next four hours. I wanted to know what it took to run a major dairy facility and how to operate big, high volume equipment. Little did I know how this would pay off in the not too distant future.

Our precious daughter, Vicki, was born on November 18, 1952. She was beautiful and perfect. We did not have a "how to" book, and Vicki must have thought she would starve before we had the sterilized formula bottles ready to go for her first feeding once we got her home. We had no insurance at the time, and it took many years to pay off the hospital bills, but Vicki was worth it many times over and she still is.

I found my job at Washington Dairy was needing more and more of my time, as I was promoted to the pasteurizer's job and put in charge of the plant. I decided it was time to leave Foremost and discontinue my trips to Los Angeles five days a week. Margaret was glad to have my help in the evenings with our little one.

About this time Washington Dairy was sold to a new owner, and I was offered the opportunity to buy into the company and become a partner. I accepted and became vice president of production. What a title for this boy from Texas!

We had our second baby on June 2, 1955. Cassie was another beautiful, perfect baby girl, and this time we felt more prepared for bringing a baby home. This time we also had insurance, which helped a lot with the costs.

Six years later, I asked my partner in the spring about making plans for some time off during the summer months to spend with my family. As it was, I was working six or seven days a week. I snuck in time to visit them when I went to pick up a load of milk nearby.

My partner must have known it was coming as he had his answer ready. He said, "I don't see how we can take any time off this year." And he turned and walked out of the building to make another delivery.

I could not let this decision stand. I was hurt after our years of working non-stop together. Before he was out of sight, I was on the phone to Foremost Dairies and they had a job for me as soon as I could get there. I gave my two-week notice to my partner and told him to do with my half of the company only as his conscience would allow. Several years later, I was to get all my money back from my investment in Washington Dairy stock.

Back at Foremost I was the man with the lowest seniority, so it appeared at first as though "I had jumped from the frying pan into the fire," as they say. All the summer vacation time was taken up by the old timers with as much as four weeks' vacation apiece. I remained firm in my belief that the good and the bad things that happen to you in life can work out in a positive way if you continue to work at it. Determined to spend some long overdue time with my family that summer, I was able to trade days off with other fellow employees. I would work for them and they would work for me. I was able to get nine days off and I took my family to Huntington, Utah to Ezra Harrison's Lazy Daze Ranch for a nice summer vacation. We had a great time! My hard work and patience had paid off.

I bid on a relief job where I bounced around working all three shifts each week: graveyard, swing, and days. I could now do all the most difficult jobs in the processing department, including the foreman's job. My resume was growing!

All the while, I was also working at other local small dairies, learning new systems and new machinery. As I was the relief foreman at Foremost, I knew could be criticized by the union for working at a non-union plant. It took only a couple of weeks and the plant manager called me into his office and asked me if I was working at another milk plant. I answered honestly. He stated that I could not get ahead at Foremost if I was going to continue to do so. It was real quiet for a moment. I asked if he had anything else to say. He did not. So I got up and walked out of his office.

In 1965, the Watts riots in Los Angeles were getting completely out of control in South Central, with buildings, houses, businesses and everything else in between burning. On our shift breaks at Foremost Dairy, we would go on the roof of the building and watch as everything progressively got worse. We wondered if we would be able to get home after our shift, or even back to work the next day. Injured people, some with broken arms and bodies beaten to a pulp, many bleeding profusely were walking north out of South Central. It was bad and getting worse by the hour. As we watched the fires grow to the east, west, and south of the plant, suddenly the huge lumberyard to the north of us was torched. We were surrounded by chaos. I knew I needed to get out of there, not only safely home that night but also safely to a new job.

Then as it almost always has been for me, when things appear to get real bad, there has almost always been a light at the end of the tunnel. I saw an advertisement in the newspaper in the lunch room at Foremost. Alpha Beta stores in La Habra was looking for experienced personnel to staff their new state-of-the-art milk processing plant. I filled out an application, turned in my resume, and waited. One whole month I waited. Finally I was called to have an interview at Alpha Beta. I arrived almost an hour early and sat in my car, ensuring I was not late for my interview time. The creamery manager, Charlie Sapp, and plant superintendent, Jim Prince picked me up in the lobby and escorted me to the cafeteria. We had coffee and just sat and talked for about a half hour. With no further ado, they asked me how soon I could start work. I told them I would like to give one month notice to Foremost Dairy, as I had learned so much at Foremost and had been treated so well there. Charlie (as he asked me to call him from that day forward) told me, "Give Foremost one week!"

In just one week, as Charlie had suggested, I started at Alpha Beta. I was in charge of the plant but I was only a pasteurizer reporting to the plant superintendent. After two or three years, this superintendent left the company and he was replaced by someone with no milk production experience. I was relied on to run the plant, even without the title of superintendent. I was ready and did not disappoint.

It happened then that my new boss moved up to director of manufacturing. One day I was called into the office for a meeting with the director and the vice president of Alpha Beta. I was asked if I would like to have the plant superintendent's job. Unsure, I asked how long I had to decide. I knew this new job would mean a suit and tie and more time behind a desk. They gave me two weeks to decide.

After two weeks, I accepted.

By 1979, our once modern, state-of-the-art, milk production facility was outdated and needed major changes to continue to be productive and profitable. Charlie and I wrote a report laying out all the areas in the facility that were deficient, including the reasons and the costs to correct the deficiencies.

While we were asking for upgrades, we said to each other, "Why not ask for more?" We added to our list equipment to manufacture fruit drinks (including a liquid sugar tank so we could meter the sugar and save costs), an additional 30,000-gallon raw milk storage tank, and two new blow mold machines to manufacture plastic gallon jugs. We would then have the ability to almost double our capacity. The total cost was estimated at two million dollars. Well worth it, we thought, and the president agreed. In fact he signed off on our request the same day.

I contacted my suppliers, installers, and my chief engineer at Alpha Beta and with everyone's input, I set six months as our completion date. Considering all we had to accomplish, the difficulties involved completing this enormous undertaking while producing over 100,000 gallons of product and shipping it out every day was an enormous undertaking. No one believed we would reach this goal.

I scheduled a weekly meeting each Monday morning at 8:00am and usually asked just one question, "Are we on schedule?" If not, everyone knew we would work the following weekend to get back on schedule. We never had to work on the weekends though. I can only guess my threat of overtime and long weekend hours saved us thousands of dollars.

The deadline came and we were up and running on all systems, a new empty case conveyor over 1,000 feet long, new blow molders, new gallon fillers, a new 7,000 gallon per hour high temperature short time, two new valve clusters and computerized cleaning systems, and a CIP (clean in place) for pre-programmed cleaning of all new and existing tanks and stainless systems. Milk deliveries to the stores had been as much as eight hours late for months. Once again deliveries were on time and we were on a roll!

After we were up and running for several days, I drove to

the plant on a Sunday and noticed I was pulling into the parking lot behind Charlie. He had been on a two-week vacation to South Dakota. I followed him to his parking spot and he came running over to my car with the biggest smile on his face.

"You did it, you did it!" Charlie cheered. "You got the gallons of milk into our stores!"

"Did you expect that I would not have gotten the gallons to the stores?" I asked with a smile. He only laughed and laughed.

Once again, hard work had paid off in the end.

12 A POEM

The following is a poem that I heard my dad recite many times and I would like to pass it along in his memory:

A fly and a flea in a flue

Were imprisoned, so what could they do?

Said the fly, "Let us flee!"

"Let us fly!" said the flea.

So they flew through a flaw in the flue.

\- Ogden Nash

Compelled by love for family, my grandfather had no time for hobbies. He often told me that his family was his hobby.

My grandfather had a strong work ethic engrained deep in his bones. No trace of laziness. He worked through his childhood, from dawn 'til dusk, year after year, home after home – cotton picking in his youth, milk production in his age. It didn't really matter what the work was, as long as there was work and a wage. And then he'd spend that money on his family.

My Poppa's back was literally broken for his family.

Childhood years in Texas were made of dirt roads and small houses, sometimes a rented room or a shared property. Those years consisted of moving from house to house just to keep up with rent or to borrow a room from extended family or a kind neighbor. Long days in cotton fields, long walks on unpaved roads, cramped spaces, and meager meals formed the years that created his depth of character and molded his soul. His crystal blue eyes had seen so much pain, so much need, and still smiled from far beneath the surface, way down to the places where he loved so completely.

Dear Poppa,

I haven't taken your lessons lightly. Thank you for sharing your stories, for teaching me to work hard and love my family. I love you, Pops, and I miss you. I'll see you one day when my work is done, and we can swap stories for all eternity.

With all my heart,

Rachael Christine

13 GOING WAY BACK: MATTIE'S STORY (STARTED IN 1969 IN HER OWN WORDS)

This following narrative was written by my great-great grandmother, Martha Ann, as a letter to her children. She was one of many children, not all of who lived a long life. She began this writing in 1969, at the age of 79, and she spent two years composing her thoughts. Her story is one of hard work and poverty, not unlike that of my grandfather's story in his early years. Her story gives depth to where my grandfather came from, who his grandparents were, and why family and hard work came first in all things.

My name is Martha Ann. My family called me Mattie during my growing up years. I was born the 7th day of January 1890, five miles south of Bonham, Texas. I was born in a log house. My father cut the logs for the log house with his own strong arms. Long before I was born, Father bought forty acres of timber land. This land would be of use. This land would help us live. He cleared the land and sold the logs in Bonham to help pay for the land. Father even dug the stumps out. We had a fireplace. Every night Father called us all in and he read the Bible and prayed. Father worked hard. He was tired at night. He went to bed and fell asleep quickly.

Sometime later, Father built on a side room. We did not have rugs of any kind, just bare board floors. Our one room log house was eighteen by twenty feet. Later on in years, Father joined a one-room shack with a porch to the log house. The porch was really more of a breeze-way. The addition became our kitchen, just fourteen by fourteen feet.

On the front he made a small bedroom and added a small porch.

My Father had a brick well dug there close to the house. That big well has been there more than eighty years and it has never gone dry. I have drawn lots of water from that well.

I lived in that old house with my folks until I was fourteen years old, the year that Florence was born. Father had the old house cleared away and in September he had a new four-room house made. The house had four porches and three fireplaces.

In our family were twelve children who lived to be grown. One brother died at eight years of age, and Albert's twin sister died at three months old. There would have been six girls and nine boys in total. I did all the washing at fourteen years old and most of the cooking. You see, I have worked ever since I was knee high to a duck.

Florence was born July 25, 1903. That was the year Father built the new house, the one with four rooms. Virgil and Florence said I was their second mother, always taking care of them. I even changed the diapers on the little ones when I was a very small girl.

Us kids walked two-and-a-half miles to school in the black mud. No pavement roads. At that time the little town was called Edhube. It had one school, two churches, and a post office in a store. Us kids didn't even have Sunday clothes. I had one pair of shoes. The boys milked the cows in a dirty lot. They got mess on their shoes and didn't have any shoes to put on to go to school. They had overalls and blue shirts. Mother made all the underclothes out of cotton flannel. I never had a pair of store-bought panties until I was married.

I was with my family and that was what mattered – family mattered.

Somehow we all had a good time and plenty to eat. Father killed eight big hogs every year. We had chickens for eggs, and when I was sixteen, I took a half bushel of eggs to the market in town. I walked and carried them, no other way to go. That is a big, heavy load of eggs for one girl carry.

Florence was born in 1903, while we were still in the old house. Vernie was the only one of the kids born in the new house. I cooked the first meal in the new house. Mother wasn't able to do any work, so it was up to me. After Father died, I helped the boys to milk the cows. They were drying up the cows to where we didn't get very much milk and butter, so the old cows mended up. That was boys for you, with no father.

Years after Father bought the first forty acres, he bought another forty acres. He cleared the land of trees and that was what we called the lower forty.

The last licking my Father gave me was over Pearl. That

was in the old house. Mother went to a neighbor's to help her have her baby. Pearl asked me for some bread. I broke a biscuit in half and gave to Pearl. She let out a big cry. Father gave me a good hard licking with a peach tree limb. I didn't slap her like Pearl said. I was hurt because I knew I didn't do anything to get such a licking. After I got over my cry I told Father I did not slap her. He said, "I'll never lick you anymore."

I remember when Luther, my brother, would swipe eggs from the henhouse and use them to buy candy. He would give me part of the candy. I never told on him, because I liked candy, too.

I remember when I was sprinkled in the Methodist Church. This was being baptized. I was only three years old. I cried when the water ran down my neck. I still have the certificate. It was in 1893, the eleventh day of August. The paper is rotten, but I still keep it.

When I was a girl at home, we didn't have bought soap. We took a bath with lye soap. And we didn't have dusting powder, we used starch. I am sure Father and Mother did their best with all us kids. Sometimes your best is all you can do, and that has to be enough.

Remember always, family matters.

When I was a little girl we didn't have store bought play things. We made our playhouses with old broken dishes. Some of those broken dishes were cups and plates to us. We had a big wood yard with several big oak trees, nice shades. One of the boys made a swing and we would see how high we could swing.

East of our house about a quarter mile was a big hog lot, about two acres. Once my cousin and I were out walking and I climbed the gate into the lot. Right there in front of me was a great big boar hog. I heard him coming before I saw him. Believe me, I got out of the pen in time. That hog would have killed me, but I just wanted to give it a try. Another time I jumped off a big haystack and almost broke my neck. You see all kids take chances. We all do dumb things.

When I was a wee little girl I didn't know about a washing machine. We had a washboard – that was a hard way to wash. First you have to pull up water from the well, then heat it up, then you have to get the soap (if you have any) and then you start to scrub. And you keep scrubbing until your arms are sore and your knuckles are raw. Clothes got so dirty out there in the fields. Sometimes we would wash clothes in the river.

Sometimes the wash pot had to be used for preparing for winter. I remember when Mother and Father would make hominy in our big wash pot outdoors. Sometimes it would be yellow corn. Mother would pack it in big churn jars. And we made green tomato pickles and put them in big stone jars, five or six gallon jars. We also made chow-chow and put it up the same way, also kraut.

Under the old house we had what we called a cellar where Mother would put canned stuff and we kept our milk in the cellar sitting in a tub of water. We changed the water every day. All the ice we had was in the wintertime.

Father was a farmer. He raised corn, cotton, wheat, and we had two big pecan trees on the lower forty. We sat by the fireplace in the wintertime and ate pecans. Those trees were still there the year I married my sweetheart. Father had planted turnips, so we ate turnips and cornbread until our bellies were stuffed. Boy, were they good! We would churn butter every day to have it on hand for our meals.

When us twelve was all at home, for breakfast we had biscuits, syrup, butter, and most of the time we had eggs. The old hens would go on a strike every now and then and stop laying eggs. We never bought any eggs though. We ate gravy and did not grumble because it wouldn't do us any good.

I sat at the end of the table where I could wait on the others, all my brothers and sisters plus Mother and Father – so I could go get hot bread and pour the milk. Then after each meal was my time to wash the dishes. Sometimes Pearl would dry the dishes. She would leave them wet so next morning I would get bawled out. If I said that it was Pearl who dried them, I got slapped in the mouth by Mother. She thought the sun and moon rose on Pearl. I got all the blame.

I had the sweetest Father in the world. It nearly killed me when he died. He was fifty-five when he died – he didn't live enough years. I miss him still. I have an enlarged picture of my Father and Mother. It was taken before my time. It sits before me on the mantel as I write.

When I was small, we still lived in the old house. Mother raised geese and she had a small pen to keep them in. While Mother picked the feathers, I had to hold the geese and they would bite me. Then I'd have to cry. This is where Mother got all the feathers to make pillows and feather beds. I still to this day have that old bed she made. It is quite old.

Sometimes I wonder how my poor Mother got along having all her children. She raised twelve to be grown and married. I did the work for Mother – washing linens, cleaning house, cooking, washing dishes. I suppose Mother didn't feel like doing very much work, so they all called on me. She kept busy, though, with her own work around the house. That's why I never went to school very much. I'm still scatterbrained and wish I had more schooling.

I can look back and see that when I did go to school, I didn't go to school clean. This day and time it's a bath every night. I can't remember ever washing my hair in the wintertime. Now I wash my hair every week.

I was eight years old when I started to school after Christmas, after my birthday. I was kept out of school off and on the first year. That year I did learn my ABCs, but I couldn't even write my name when school was out in June. Every time there was work to do Mother kept me home. That was the way I had to do until I was sixteen. The year that Vernie was born Mother was sick all the time, and I was kept out of school the whole year. Then I quit going to school altogether because I wasn't learning anything anyway. I washed for all the family. In between the big washing, I had to wash diapers – I washed it all on the washboard.

We had oil lamps and it was also my job to fill the lamps and clean the lamp globes. Mother taught me how to piece a string quilt together by hand long before I was sixteen. In the afternoons Mother had to make or mend clothes for us children and I would rock the baby in the cradle and watch her sew.

One time Mother and Aunt Dovie went to Gainsville, Texas on the train to visit her sister. I was left at home with Father. I had to cook and wash clothes. Mother was gone a whole week. Some days Father would help me cook, but mostly I made the meals. Mother had me catch a fryer chicken and kill it. I didn't break the chicken's neck though. Mother always said I choked it to death.

My father was a tall slender man with a good head of reddish hair. He was honest and well-respected. He made a good living, enough to buy sugar by the barrel – sometimes it was even brown sugar. Every day I'd get me a big lump of sugar and eat it. Us kids never got much candy. At Christmastime, Father would get a sack of apples and a bag of stick candy. Mighty few playthings that we got. We didn't have the money.

Mother would make a pound cake for Christmas. She would bake it in a big pan that we also used for cooking biscuits. No icing. Never enough sugar to make icing.

Mother and Daddy would go to Bonham in the wagon for groceries and other things. It was five miles to Bonham. Mother would leave the children with me, even a baby who was about six months old. I would give the baby milk to drink and feed him or her with a spoon. I was only fourteen or fifteen years old – I often nearly forgot my age. I learned to be a mother very young by helping my own mother.

I could go to the kitchen and cook a big meal for company, while Mother would visit with the ladies that came. After we all ate, I washed the dishes, then I'd have to take the little ones out and play with them. The company would go home. Then I'd have to wash diapers and take them out to the well, draw water and wash them out. I'd pour out the dirty water and put them in clean water and get soap and rub them on a washboard.

I am not sorry that I learned to work. All I knew was work, work, work. But it kept our family going. And family is what mattered.

14 FALLING IN LOVE

In 1908, Grandfather took me with him to Byers for a visit.
I stayed two months with Uncle Jim and Aunt Dovie down
by Byers Lake. I made a friend, Clara, who was Pearl's age
and some younger than me, but we both had a swell time
going places. Clara had a boyfriend by the name of
Abner. One day Clara and Abner made a blind date for me
on Sunday. On Saturday evening, Clara and I went for a
walk between sundown and dark. We talked quietly with
our heads bowed together.

Along the way came a young man who would be my love. I
met him there in Byers, right by the lake, the day before he

was to be my blind date on Sunday. He was farming out south of Byers and was on his way home. I didn't know what to think.

Every Sunday we went to church together – Clara and Abner King and your Daddy and me. We two couples stayed close to each other. Clara and I had a special time to be back at the house after we would go to church on Sunday night. Other days the four of us went lots of places in Byers. At that time a boy didn't have a lot of money to spend on his girl, so us four never did go anyplace fancy to eat.

I helped pay my way while I was at Aunt Dovie's house. I washed and ironed for a woman named Mrs. Tucker. I didn't lie around, even while I was on a visit. Clara didn't take hold of work like I did. I was the oldest and I had learned the meaning of hard work.

Aunt Dovie told me I could stay with them through the

early summer. Mother wrote a letter to me and told me to stay if I wanted to. Of course I wanted to. Every week I jumped in and helped Aunt Dovie with the wash – she only had a washboard, like us at home – and often Clara and I would pick cotton together. Clara cried when I left to go home.

After I got back to Mother's in July, I had to wait until Christmas to see your Daddy. He and Abner came to Bonham to see me in a nice rubbed tire buggy. It even had a top! The two boys both had their own buggy and good horses to drive. Your Daddy was the nicest boy I ever went with. He said I was the girl for him and I just laughed at him. Sounds silly, but he made me laugh.

After your Daddy came to see me that Christmas, he left Byers and went out somewhere in West Texas and got a job. He wrote to me in March 1909, and asked if I'd be his wife. I put off answering him for some time. I wanted to be sure I loved him before I said yes, but I finally did.

So in a letter we set the date: April 18, 1909. Just one month away! We were married in Mother's house at 2:30 in the afternoon by a Baptist preacher. We stayed two weeks with Mother and that was our honeymoon.

I packed up what I had and we caught a train to Wichita Falls, then went on to Byers. We lived with my grandfather for several days, then we went and stayed a while at another family's house. I got tired of staying with people, so we rented a little two-room house. We did not have much but we was happy and that meant everything.

15 REAL LIFE AND RAISING A FAMILY

The first year we were married, we moved to Erick, Oklahoma in a covered wagon, almost 200 miles. We were a heavy load, also pulling a buggy behind the wagon. We hadn't drove very far before your Daddy got out to walk and drive the horses. He got too close to the wagon and the front wheel ran over his foot and mashed off his big toenail. He was in so much pain and could barely walk.

We stopped at a house of someone Dad knew and had his foot dressed, then we went on our way again. It took us eleven days to make that trip. I got sick on the road and the last night we camped out, there came a big snow. We only had to drive four or five miles farther to our one-room house. Our very own house!

There wasn't any windows in the house. I stayed with a neighbor and Dad went into Erick and got windows and put them in. In two or three days, he was home. It wasn't easy but we were finally together in a house of our own.

We lost our first baby girl the next winter in Erick. I nearly died. We moved to Denton, Texas soon after that winter.

Your Daddy dug a well and put up a windmill. There was an old half dug-out and that's where we put the horses out of the wind in the winter. Now I can look back and that was a horrible place to live. We were so happy to be together though.

Sometime toward the end of January 1910, we was both working. Your Daddy ran a bundle wagon and I cooked at the cook shack. I got $2.00 per day and he got $1.50 per day. I liked the work. I had twenty-five men to cook for three times a day.

That same year in the fall, we picked cotton just a mile from our house. I was expecting Edna Mae in March of the next year and those days were long and hot. We each picked 100 pounds of cotton a day. Our baby girl, Edna Mae, was born the 27th of March, 1911, in Denton, Texas.

We stayed in Denton one season – made one crop of corn, but no cotton – and then moved to Ponder, Texas, just sixteen miles from Denton. A man there rented us a house. We put in a big cotton crop and corn, but we didn't have a good harvest that summer. We loaded up in the fall of 1912, caught the train, and went back to Byers. We found a small house and settled down to raise our children.

The little town of Byers, Texas became home for many, many years to come, for your generation and the next.

RACHAEL WOODALL

POPPA AND HIS GREAT-GRANDDAUGHTER, IRIS PAISLEY
JUNE 2007

RACHAEL WOODALL

ABOUT THE AUTHOR

Rachael Woodall was born and raised in Southern California. She
moved with her husband, Jason, to South Carolina and then Ohio
in 2011 where they could raise their children at a slower pace with
lots of land and even cows next door. Rachael graduated from
Brown University in Rhode Island with a degree in Comparative
Literature. She taught high school, coached basketball, and earned
her Masters in Cross-Cultural Education. She and her husband now
homeschool their three children, Iris, Jonas, and Eliza. They like to
share stories and read lots and lots of books.

Made in the USA
San Bernardino, CA
07 January 2019